Mediterran Indian Salads

Cookbook

This book contains low-fat, quick and easy recipes for beginners, ideated to boost your lifestyle from the awakening and balance your daily supply. Mix European and Asian kitchen to amaze your friends and empower your skills!

Kumar Ortega

Table of Contents

Welcome, dear reader!

This is my purpose to you.

This cookbook is a creation born from a researcher of the wellness. It's finalized to increase your energies and to let you live a happier life, without the heaviness of the modern kitchen.

In this book, you'll find my knowledge on how to keep your body and mind faculties active, productive and efficient.

Jump into a world of good habits and natural foods, if you want to discover the real deepness of your overall wellness.

Nevertheless, you'll learn new ideas, discover tastes of all around the world and change your meal plan in better.

Each of these dishes is thought to:

1 - Let you wake up full of energies and keep this boost for all day long

Thanks to light and natural greens as dinner and a high nutrient supply as brunch, you'll sleep better and be full of energies during the day.

2 - Lose the excessive weight and keep your moral up

As soon as you start to eat better and do physical activity, the leftover fat will disappear from your body and your image will finally become as you wish!

3 - Improve your skills and surprise your friends

Learn some new recipes taken from the worldwide tradition and twisted by a proper chef, only to let you discover modern tastes.

Mediterranean Salads

Chicken Salad

Serves 8 pax

Ingredients

- A pinch of Black pepper
- 0.5 cup lemon juice
- 0.25 cups yogurt
- 0.25 cups mayonnaise
- 2 stalks Celery
- 2 Green onions
- 2 cups cooked chicken breast
- 1 medium Fuji apple
- 3 Tbsp walnuts

Procedure

1. Mix the chicken, green onions, walnuts, apple, and celery.
2. In another container, thoroughly combine the mayonnaise with the lemon juice, pepper, and yogurt.
3. Combine each of the components and stir thoroughly to serve.
4. Enjoy this chicken salad on a bed of lettuce, or with bread or crackers, or as the filling to a wrap.

Tomatoes and Mozzarella Polenta

Serves 6 pax

Ingredients

- 2 pounds cherry tomatoes, halved
- 2 garlic cloves, sliced thin
- 2 tablespoons shredded fresh basil
- 3 ounces fresh mozzarella cheese
- 3 tablespoons extra-virgin olive oil
- A pinch of red pepper flakes
- A pinch of sugar
- Salt and pepper

Procedure

1. Cook oil, garlic, pepper flakes, and sugar in 12-inch non-stick frying pan on moderate to high heat until aromatic and sizzling, about 1 minute.
2. Mix in tomatoes and cook until just starting to soften, about 1 minute.
3. Sprinkle with salt and pepper to taste.
4. Spoon mixture over individual portions of polenta and top with mozzarella and basil.
5. Serve.

Sprouts Salad

Serves 4 pax

Ingredients

- 2 cups sprouts
- 2 teaspoons grated gingerroot
- 6 cups baby greens
- 3 tablespoons soy sauce
- 1/4 cup rice vinegar
- 1 tablespoon sugar
- 2 tablespoons vegetable oil

Procedure

1. In a big container whisk together the vinegar, fish sauce, vegetable oil, sugar, and gingerroot.
2. Put in the sprouts, toss to coat, and let marinate for half an hour.
3. Put in the greens and toss until well blended.
4. Serve.

Free Salad

Serves 6 pax

Ingredients

- 1/2 cup Tahini-Lemon Dressing
- 1/2 cups whole freekeh
- 1/2 pounds butternut squash, peeled, seeded, and cut into 1/2-inch pieces
- 1/2 teaspoon ground fenugreek
- 1/3 cup golden raisins
- 1/3 cup walnuts, toasted and chopped
- 1 cup coarsely chopped cilantro
- 1 tablespoon extra-virgin olive oil
- Salt and pepper to taste

Procedure

1. Place oven rack on the lowest position and pre-heat your oven to 450 degrees. Toss squash with oil and fenugreek and sprinkle with salt and pepper.

2. Arrange squash in one layer in rimmed baking sheet and roast until thoroughly browned and tender, 30 to 35 minutes, stirring halfway through roasting; allow to cool to room temperature.

3. In the meantime, bring 4 quarts water to boil in a Dutch oven. Put in freekeh and 1 tablespoon salt, return to boil, and cook until grains are tender, 30 to 45 minutes.

4. Drain freekeh, move to big container, and allow to cool completely, about fifteen minutes.

5. Mix raisins and 1/4 cup hot tap water in a small-sized container and allow to sit till they become tender, approximately five minutes; drain raisins.

6. Put in squash, raisins, dressing, cilantro, and walnuts to a container with freekeh and gently toss.

7. Sprinkle with salt and pepper to taste. Serve.

Wheat Berry Salad

Serves 6 pax

Ingredients

- 1/4 cup pine nuts, toasted
- 1/2 cup fresh parsley leaves
- 1 small shallot, minced
- 1 teaspoon Dijon mustard
- 1 teaspoon honey
- 2 cups wheat berries
- 1/2 cup goat cheese, crumbled
- 2 tablespoons balsamic vinegar
- 2 tablespoons extra-virgin olive oil
- 8 ounces figs, cut into 1/2-inch pieces
- Salt and pepper

Procedure

1. Bring 4 quarts water to boil in a Dutch oven. Put in wheat berries and 11/2 teaspoons salt, return to boil, and cook until soft but still chewy, 60 to 70 minutes.
2. Drain wheat berries, spread onto rimmed baking sheet, and allow to cool completely, about fifteen minutes.
3. Beat vinegar, shallot, mustard, honey, 1/4 teaspoon salt, and 1/4 teaspoon pepper together in a big container. Whisking continuously, slowly drizzle in oil.
4. Put in wheat berries, figs, parsley, and pine nuts and toss gently to combine. Sprinkle with salt and pepper to taste.
5. Move to serving platter and drizzle with goat cheese.
6. Serve.

Broccoli and Spinaches Salad

Serves 6 pax

Ingredients

- 1 tsp black pepper
- 0.5 clove Garlic
- 1 lemon juice and zest
- 1 tsp Poppy seeds
- 4 sprigs dill
- 0.5 cups Greek yogurt
- 0.25 cups buttermilk
- 0.25 cups sunflower seeds
- 0.5 Avocado
- 0.25 cups blueberries
- 0.25 cups feta cheese
- 1 cup broccoli
- 8 oz baby spinach

Procedure

1. Toss the spinach, avocado, broccoli, feta cheese, blueberries, and sunflower seeds in a large mixing container.

2. Use your blender to mix the lemon juice, buttermilk, yogurt, garlic, lemon zest, dill or other herb, poppy seeds, and pepper until smooth and combined.

3. Pour the delicious dressing over the salad. Gently toss to combine the fixings and serve promptly for freshness.

4. Serve.

Greens and Pecans Salad

Ingredients

- 1 Tbsp Brown sugar blend
- 1 Tbsp Water
- 0.5 cups Pecan halves
- 2 tsp Trans fat-free margarine
- 0.25 tsp Cinnamon
- 0.25 cups Vinaigrette salad dressing
- A pinch of Cayenne pepper
- 0.25 tsp Cumin
- 7 cups Spring mix lettuce
- 2 oz Chèvre goat

Procedure

1. Set out a piece of waxed paper.

2. Use the medium temperature setting to toast the pecans. Stir often, about every four minutes.

3. Measure and add the margarine. Stir another minute until the nuts begin to darken.

4. Add the Splenda, water, cinnamon, cumin, and cayenne pepper. Cook, constantly stirring, until the sauce thickens or for about one to two minutes.

5. Evenly spread the sauce as it thickens to cover the nuts.

6. Spread the pecans on the waxed paper. Separate the nuts with a fork. Allow cooling. Stir together the lettuce, goat cheese, and pecans.

7. Spritz a portion of the dressing over the top, tossing until everything is evenly coated.

Turkey and Almonds Salad

Serves 4 pax

Ingredients

- 7 oz Oven roasted deli turkey breast
- 1.5 Tbsp Olive oil
- 0.33 cups Balsamic vinegar
- 0.33 cups feta cheese
- 2 Tbsp Almonds
- 5.5 oz Baby spinach and spring mix blend
- 1 small Apple
- 0.5 cups Dried cranberries
- 0.25 cups Dry roasted pepitas

Procedure

1. Mix the spinach blend, almonds, pepitas, cranberries, apple, feta, and turkey in a mixing container.
2. Using a smaller container, combine the vinegar and oil.
3. Sprinkle the dressing over the salad and thoroughly toss to cover before serving.

Greek Orzo Salad

Serves 6 pax

Ingredients

- 1/2 cup chopped fresh basil
- 2 cups orzo
- 2 garlic cloves, minced
- 2 cups baby arugula
- 1/4 cup extra-virgin olive oil
- 1/4 cup pine nuts, toasted
- 1/2 cup pitted kalamata olives, halved
- 1 ounce Parmesan cheese, grated
- 2 tablespoons balsamic vinegar
- Salt and pepper

Procedure

1. Bring 2 quarts water to boil in large pot. Put in orzo and 2 teaspoons salt and cook, stirring frequently, until al dente. Drain orzo and move to rimmed baking sheet.
2. Toss with 1 tablespoon oil and allow to cool completely, about fifteen minutes.
3. Beat remaining 3 tablespoons oil, vinegar, garlic, 1/2 teaspoon salt, and 1/2 teaspoon pepper together in a big container.
4. Put in arugula, Parmesan, tomatoes, olives, basil, pine nuts, and orzo and gently toss to combine.
5. Sprinkle with salt and pepper to taste. Let salad sit until flavors blend, approximately half an hour.
6. Serve, drizzled with extra oil.

Cucumber and Peanuts Salad

Serves 5 pax

Ingredients

- 1/2 cup finely chopped fresh cilantro
- 1/2 cup roasted and lightly salted peanuts
- 1/8 teaspoon ground asafoetida
- 1/4 teaspoon salt
- 1 teaspoon black mustard seeds
- 2 teaspoons Marathi Curry Powder with Coconut and Sesame Seeds
- 1 fresh green chile pepper, minced with seeds
- 1 pound Armenian or any seedless cucumbers
- 1 tablespoon minced fresh curry leaves
- 1 tablespoon peanut oil

Procedure

1. In a serving container, combine the cucumbers, peanuts, cilantro, green chile pepper and salt.

2. Heat the oil in a small-sized non-stick saucepan using moderate to high heat and put in the mustard seeds; they should splutter when they touch the hot oil, so cover the pan and decrease the heat until the spluttering diminishes.

3. Swiftly put in the curry powder, asafoetida, and curry leaves, and stir for a few seconds.

4. Move to the salad. Mix thoroughly and serve.

5. Put in the spices just before you serve, or the salt will draw out the juices from the ingredients and make the salad too liquid.

Red Lentils and Cucumber Salad

Serves 5 pax

Ingredients

- 1/2 teaspoon black mustard seeds
- 2 pounds pickling or seedless cucumbers
- 2 tablespoons finely chopped fresh cilantro
- 4 scallions, finely chopped
- 1/2 teaspoon cumin seeds
- 1/2 teaspoon salt
- 1 tablespoon vegetable oil
- 1/2 cup red lentils (dhulli masoor dal), sorted, washed and soaked in water to cover approximately two hours, then drained
- 1/2 teaspoon crudely ground black pepper
- 1 teaspoon peeled minced fresh ginger
- 2 tablespoons fresh lemon juice

Procedure

1. In a serving container, combine the dal, cucumbers, scallions, and cilantro.

2. Heat the oil in a small-sized non-stick saucepan using moderate to high heat and add all the spices; they should sizzle when they touch the hot oil.

3. Swiftly put in the ginger, stir for a few seconds, then put in the lemon juice and salt.

4. Move to the salad, mix thoroughly and serve.

Daikon and Peanuts Salad

Serves 5 pax

Ingredients

- 1 cup finely chopped daikon radishes
- 1 fresh green chile pepper, minced with seeds
- 1/2 cup raw shelled peanuts, red skin on
- 2 teaspoons Chaat Masala
- 10 scallions, white parts only, thinly chopped
- 1 cup finely chopped daikon or red radish leaves
- 1 tablespoon fresh lime or lemon juice
- 2 cups sprouted green mung beans

Procedure

1. In a small-sized cast-iron or non-stick skillet, roast the peanuts, stirring and swaying the pan, over moderate heat until they are golden.
2. Allow to cool, then grind crudely with a mortar and pestle or a spice grinder.
3. In a serving container, combine the radishes, radish leaves, mung dal, scallions, chile pepper, and ground peanuts.
4. Put in the chaat masala and lime juice and toss to mix.
5. Serve at room temperature.

Eggs Salad

Serves 5 pax

Ingredients

- 1/2 cup plain Yogurt Cheese
- 1 tablespoon sesame seeds
- 1/4 cup finely chopped fresh cilantro
- 1 teaspoon ground cumin seeds
- 2 green chile peppers, minced with seeds
- 4 large eggs
- 1/4 teaspoon salt
- 1 tablespoon peeled minced fresh ginger
- 1 teaspoon Basic Curry Powder

Procedure

1. In a moderate-sized saucepan, place the eggs in water to cover by 2 inches and bring to a boil using high heat.
2. Decrease the heat to medium, cover the pan and simmer until hard-boiled, approximately ten to twelve minutes.
3. Allow to cool or plunge into cold water, shell them, then cut finely.
4. Put the eggs in a big serving container, stir in all the rest of the ingredients and serve.

Tomatoes Salad

Serves 5 pax

Ingredients

- 1 teaspoon black mustard seeds
- 1 teaspoon cumin seeds
- 2 pounds firm vine-ripened tomatoes of mixed colors, crudely chopped
- 3 cups mixed baby lettuce, mesclun, or other mixed greens
- 7 cherry or pear-shaped tomatoes of mixed colors
- 1/8 teaspoon ground asafoetida
- 1 fresh green chile pepper, minced with seeds
- 1 tablespoon olive oil
- 2 tablespoons fresh lemon juice
- 2 tablespoons minced fresh curry leaves

Procedure

1. Line a serving platter with the lettuce. Keeping a large non-stick wok or saucepan tilted to one side, heat the oil and put in the cumin and mustard seeds; they should sizzle instantly when they touch the hot oil.

2. Lay the pan flat, and swiftly Put in the green chile pepper, curry leaves, asafoetida and lemon juice and cook 1 minute.

3. Put in the tomatoes and stir softly until heated through, but still firm, approximately a minute or two. Move to the lettuce-lined platter.

4. Serve.

Pan-Fried Tomatoes Salad

Serves 5 pax

Ingredients

- 1/2 teaspoon salt
- 1 tablespoon fresh lemon juice
- 1/4 cup finely chopped fresh cilantro, with soft stems
- 1 tablespoon peanut oil
- 4 large unripe green tomatoes (about 11/2 pounds), each cut into 8 wedges
- 1/2 teaspoon Chaat Masala
- 1 tablespoon ground coriander

Procedure

1. Lay the tomato wedges in a single layer in a big nonstick skillet.
2. Drizzle the oil over them and cook using moderate to high heat until the bottoms are golden, approximately four minutes.
3. Turn each piece over, sprinkle the coriander and salt over them, and cook until the other side is golden, approximately two minutes.
4. Put in the lemon juice and cilantro, very cautiously mix everything together, and cook approximately half a minute.
5. Move to a serving dish, sprinkle with the chaat masala before you serve.

Tomatoes and Scallion Salad

Serves 5 pax

Ingredients

- 1/4 cup packaged fine sev noodles
- 1/4 teaspoon salt
- Crudely ground black pepper, to taste
- 2 tablespoons minced fresh cilantro leaves
- 8 small, firm, vine-ripened tomatoes, cut into thin wedges
- 12 scallions, white and light green parts only, thinly chopped
- 1 small lime
- 1 tablespoon minced fresh mint leaves

Procedure

1. Put the tomato wedges on a large serving platter and scatter the scallions over them.
2. Slice the lime in half and microwave on high approximately half a minute.
3. Squeeze 1 or both the halves over the tomatoes.
4. Top with salt, black pepper, cilantro, mint, and sev noodles before you serve.

Broccoli and Cabbage Salad

Serves 5 pax

Ingredients

- 1/2 teaspoon salt
- 1 cup broccoli florets
- 1 cup finely shredded romaine lettuce
- 1/4 cup finely chopped fresh cilantro, with soft stems
- 1/2 cup grated daikon radish
- 2 teaspoons multi-colored peppercorns
- 2 cups finely shredded green cabbage
- 1/2 cup yogurt, whisked until the desired smoothness is achieved
- 1 tablespoon peeled minced fresh ginger
- 1 teaspoon fresh lime juice
- 10 small cherry or pear-shaped tomatoes, halved

Procedure

1. In a large serving container, combine the cabbage, lettuce, broccoli, tomatoes, daikon radish, and cilantro.
2. In a small-sized container, combine the yogurt, ginger, lime juice, salt, and pepper, and add to the salad.
3. Roast the peppercorns.
4. Toss the salad well then garnish with a few coarse grindings from the peppermill.
5. Serve.

Cabbage and Onion Salad

Serves 5 pax

Ingredients

- 1 green bell pepper, cut into thin matchsticks
- 1 small red onion, thinly chopped
- 12 fresh curry leaves
- 2 cups shredded green cabbage
- 3 small tomatoes, cut into thin wedges
- 4 whole dried red chile peppers
- 1/4 teaspoon salt
- 1 tablespoon coconut or peanut oil
- 1 tablespoon distilled white vinegar
- 1 tablespoon sesame seeds
- 1 teaspoon mustard seeds

Procedure

1. Roast the sesame seeds. Next, in a big serving container, combine the onion, cabbage, bell pepper, and tomatoes.

2. Heat the oil in a small-sized non-stick wok or saucepan using moderate to high heat and put in the mustard seeds; they should splutter when they touch the hot oil, so cover the pan and decrease the heat until the spluttering diminishes.

3. Swiftly put in the red chile peppers and curry leaves and cook, stirring, approximately half a minute.

4. Put in the vinegar and salt and move the mixture to the salad. Toss well, and garnish with sesame seeds.

5. Refrigerate up to two hours before you serve chilled.

Lemon and Cabbages Salad

Serves 5 pax

Ingredients

- 1/2 teaspoon salt
- 2 whole dried red chili peppers
- 2 fresh curry leaves
- 1 tablespoon peanut oil
- 2 cups finely shredded green cabbage
- 1/2 teaspoon black mustard seeds
- 1/2 teaspoon cumin seeds
- 2 tablespoons fresh lemon juice

Procedure

1. Heat the oil in a big non-stick wok or skillet over moderate heat and put in the mustard and cumin seeds; they should sizzle when they touch the hot oil.

2. Swiftly put in the red chili peppers and the fresh curry leaves and stir a few seconds, then, put in the cabbage and cook briefly, maximum ten to fifteen seconds. If you see the cabbage wilting, move it to a big container instantly.

3. Put in the lemon juice and salt. Toss and serve instantly.

Yogurt Coleslaw

Serves 5 pax

Ingredients

- 1/2 cup finely chopped fresh cilantro
- 1/2 teaspoon freshly ground black pepper
- 1/2 teaspoon salt
- 12 scallions, minced
- 1/4 cup almond slivers
- 1 cup finely diced bell peppers of mixed colors
- 1 tablespoon peeled minced fresh ginger
- 1 teaspoon Chaat Masala
- 2 cups finely shredded green cabbage
- 2 cups finely shredded purple cabbage
- 1 cup yogurt, whisked
- 1 fresh serrano pepper, minced, with seeds
- 1 tablespoon lemon juice
- 1 tablespoon minced fresh mint leaves

Procedure

1. In a moderate-sized container, combine the yogurt, lime juice, serrano pepper, ginger, chaat masala, black pepper, and salt.

2. Put the green and purple cabbage, bell pepper, scallions, cilantro, and mint in a big container.

3. Put in the yogurt dressing and toss to mix thoroughly.

4. Move to a wide serving container, garnish with the almonds before you serve.

Cashew Carrots Salad

Serves 5 pax

Ingredients

- 1/2 teaspoon salt
- 2 tablespoons fresh lemon juice
- 20 raw cashews, crudely chopped
- 1 pound carrots, peeled and grated
- 1 tablespoon finely chopped fresh curry leaves
- 1 teaspoon black mustard seeds
- 1/8 teaspoon ground asafoetida
- 1/4 cup grated fresh coconut
- 1/2 cup finely chopped fresh cilantro
- 1 teaspoon cumin seeds
- 1 teaspoon peanut oil
- 2 green chile peppers, halved lengthwise

Procedure

1. In a large serving container, combine the carrots, coconut, cashews, cilantro, salt, and lemon juice.

2. In a small saucepan, heat the oil over moderate heat and put in the mustard and cumin seeds; they should splutter when they touch the hot oil, so cover the pan until the spluttering diminishes.

3. Put in the curry leaves, asafoetida, and green chile peppers and cook, stirring, approximately one minute.

4. Move to the carrots, stirring softly to mix.

5. Serve at room temperature or refrigerate at least two hours to serve chilled.

Peanuts Salad

Serves 5 pax

Ingredients

- 1/2 cup orange juice
- 1 cup finely chopped, firm tomato
- 1/4 teaspoon salt
- 1/2 cup finely chopped fresh cilantro
- 3 teaspoons Chaat Masala
- 4 scallions, finely chopped
- 1 teaspoon ground dried mint leaves
- 2 cups raw peanuts, red skins removed
- 2 tablespoons fresh lemon juice

Procedure

1. In a moderate-sized container mix the orange juice, 1 teaspoon chaat masala, mint, salt, and peanuts.
2. Cover and marinate in the refrigerator, 2 to four hours.
3. Move the peanuts to a large non-stick skillet and cook using moderate to high heat, stirring, approximately two to three minutes, then decrease the heat to medium and cook until most of the liquid evaporates.
4. Move to a serving container and allow to cool down.
5. Next, stir in the tomato, scallions, cilantro, and lemon juice.
6. Sprinkle the rest of the chaat masala on top and serve.

Tomato and Cucumber Salad

Serves 5 pax

Ingredients

- 1/2 pound Armenian cucumbers, finely chopped
- 1 fresh green chile pepper, minced with seeds
- 1/4 cup finely chopped fresh cilantro
- 2 teaspoons Chaat Masala
- 2 cups finely chopped romaine lettuce
- 1/4 teaspoon ground ajwain seeds
- 1 pound yellow tomatoes, finely chopped
- 2 tablespoons fresh lime or lemon juice
- 2 tablespoons peeled minced fresh ginger

Procedure

1. Mix everything in a big container.

2. Tweak the seasonings to your taste and serve.

3. Put in the spices just before you serve, or the salt in the chaat masala will draw out the juices from the ingredients and make the salad too liquidy.

Berries Salad

Ingredients

- 3 cups fresh mixed berries, such as raspberries and blackberries
- 1 cup chopped fresh mint leaves
- 1 teaspoon Chaat Masala

Procedure

1. Rinse and drain the berries, blot with paper towels, then place on a towel and allow to air-dry until as dry as possible.
2. In the meantime, ready the chaat masala. Move to a serving container, put in the chaat masala, and toss lightly.
3. Garnish with mint leaves and serve.

Black-Eyed Peas Salad

Serves 5 pax

Ingredients

- 1 tablespoon ground coriander
- 1 tablespoon minced fresh mint leaves
- 1/2 cup yogurt, whisked
- 1/2 teaspoon Chaat Masala
- 1/2 teaspoon ground cumin
- 5 scallions, white parts only, minced
- 1/4 teaspoon ground black salt
- 1 teaspoon cumin seeds
- 1 teaspoon salt
- 2 tablespoons fresh lime juice

- 3 cups outer leaves of radicchio or butter lettuce,
- 1/4 teaspoon ground turmeric
- 1/2 teaspoon ground paprika
- 1 cup black-eyed peas, sorted, washed, and soaked overnight in 2 cups water
- 1 fresh green chile pepper, minced with seeds
- 1 large firm tomato, finely chopped
- 1 tablespoon peanut oil
- 1 tablespoon peeled minced fresh ginger

Procedure

1. Place the black-eyed peas and soaking water, turmeric, and salt in a moderate-sized non-stick saucepan and bring to a boil using high heat.
2. Decrease the heat to moderate to low, cover the pan, and simmer until all the water evaporates, leaving behind beans that are soft and tender but not broken, approximately one hour. (Pour in additional water during cooking, if needed.)

3. Move to a container and stir in the tomato, scallions, ginger, mint, green chile pepper, and lime juice. Allow to cool, then stir in the yogurt.

4. Heat the oil in a small-sized non-stick saucepan using moderate to high heat and put in the cumin seeds; they should sizzle when they touch the hot oil.

5. Swiftly put in the coriander, ground cumin, black salt, and paprika, stir for approximately half a minute, and move to the black-eyed peas.

6. Mix well. Present the salad in radicchio or butter lettuce cups or mounded over a bed of shredded greens. Garnish with chaat masala before you serve at room temperature or chilled.

Fruity Salad

Serves 5 pax

Ingredients

- 1 cup strawberries, crudely chopped
- 1 green chile pepper, minced with seeds
- 1/2 cup finely chopped fresh cilantro
- 1 cup cherries, pitted and halved
- 2 teaspoons Chaat Masala
- 2 pounds mixed fruits, such as peaches, nectarines, and apricots, pitted
- 1 large mango, peeled and crudely chopped
- 1 tablespoon minced fresh mint leaves
- 1 tablespoon peeled minced fresh ginger
- 2 tablespoons fresh lime or lemon juice

Procedure

1. In a big serving container, combine the peaches, nectarines, apricots, and mango.
2. Remove approximately 1 cup of the mixed fruits, mash coarsely, and return to the container.
3. Stir in the cherries and strawberries, then put in the ginger, cilantro, mint, chili pepper, lime juice, and chaat masala.
4. Mix thoroughly and serve.

Beans Salad

Serves 5 pax

Ingredients

- 1/3 cup finely chopped fresh cilantro
- 5 scallions, finely chopped
- 1/4 cup any south chutney of your choice
- 1/2 teaspoon salt
- 1 medium tomato, finely chopped
- 2 teaspoons Chaat Masala
- 1 cup dried dew beans (muth dal), sorted and washed in 3 to 4 changes of water
- 1/2 cup dried split yellow chickpeas (channa dal), sorted and washed in 3 to 4 changes of water
- 1/2 teaspoon cayenne pepper
- 2 tablespoons peeled minced fresh ginger
- 3 tablespoons fresh lime juice
- 4 cups water

Procedure

1. Place both dals, the cayenne pepper, salt, and water in a moderate-sized saucepan and bring to a boil using high heat.
2. Decrease the heat to moderate to low, cover the pan, and simmer until all the water has evaporated, approximately 25 minutes, leaving behind a soft cooked, dry dal.
3. Stir in the ginger and allow to cool down.
4. When cool, stir in the tomato, scallions, lime juice, cilantro, and chaat masala.
5. Move to a serving dish, drizzle with south chutney before you serve, if possible, at room temperature.

Vermicelli Salad

Serves 5 pax

Ingredients

- 2 cups sprouted mixed dals and grains, such as green mung beans, green and red lentils, and whole-wheat kernels
- 1 fresh green chile pepper, minced with seeds
- 1 teaspoon New Delhi Street Food Masala
- 1/4 cup finely chopped fresh cilantro
- 1 cup packaged potato vermicelli (aalu bhujia)
- 2 tablespoons fresh lime juice

Procedure

1. Ready the sprouted dals and grains in advance. Ready the masala.
2. Next, mix everything in a big serving container and serve instantly, before the vermicelli gets soggy.

Indian Salads

Chicory Salad

Serves 4 pax

Ingredients

- 4 heads of chicory
- 6 ounces blue cheese
- 4 ounces radishes
- 3 ounces walnut halves
- 1 green pepper
- 2 sticks of celery

Procedure

1. Clean and trim chicory, chop coarsely.
2. Put the chicory and flaked cheese in a large bowl.
3. Add pepper, celery and sliced radish, mix thoroughly.
4. Toss with dressing until well coated.

Parsi Beans Salad

Serves 5 pax

Ingredients

- 1 small onion, finely chopped
- 1 tablespoon Parsi Garam Masala with Star Anise
- 1/2 cup finely chopped fresh cilantro
- 1 tomato, cut into wedges
- 2 tablespoons peanut oil
- 2 tablespoons water
- 1 fresh green chile pepper, minced with seeds
- 1 tablespoon sprouted fenugreek seeds
- 1 teaspoon salt or to taste
- 2 tablespoons fresh lime juice
- 4 cups sprouted mixed dals, such as mung beans and green lentils

Procedure

1. Heat the oil in a moderate-sized non-stick wok or saucepan using moderate to high heat and cook the onion, stirring, until a golden color is achieved, approximately five minutes.
2. Put in the garam masala, green chile pepper, and cilantro, and cook, stirring, approximately one minute.
3. Put in the sprouted dals, fenugreek seeds, salt, and water, and decrease the heat to moderate to low.
4. Cover the pan and cook from 3 to ten minutes, depending on the desired softness. Stir in the lime juice.
5. Move to a serving platter, garnish with tomato wedges and serve warm or at room temperature.

Red Beans Salad

Serves 5 pax

Ingredients

- 1 (1-inch) stick cinnamon, broken lengthwise
- 1 cup dried red or pinto beans, sorted, washed and soaked overnight in 2 cups water
- 2 black cardamom pods
- 2 tablespoons peeled minced fresh ginger
- 2 tablespoons Tamarind Paste
- 1 fresh green chile pepper, minced with seeds
- 1 large clove fresh garlic, minced
- 1 tablespoon minced fresh mint leaves
- 1/4 cup finely chopped fresh cilantro
- 1/4 cup yogurt, whisked
- 1/2 teaspoon cumin seeds
- 1 teaspoon Chaat Masala
- 1 teaspoon salt

Procedure

1. Place the dal and the soaking water, garlic, cardamom pods, cinnamon, and salt in a moderate-sized nonstick saucepan and bring to a boil using high heat.

2. Decrease the heat to moderate to low, cover the pan, and simmer until all the water evaporates, leaving behind beans that are soft and tender but not broken, approximately one hour. (Pour in additional water during cooking, if needed.) Move to a serving container.

3. In a small-sized container, combine the cumin seeds, yogurt, tamarind, ginger, green chile pepper, and chaat masala.

4. Put into the cooked beans and mix thoroughly, adjusting the seasonings, if needed.

5. Move to a serving dish, stir in the cilantro and mint leaves before you serve, if possible, at room temperature.

Tomatoes and Soy-Beans Salad

Serves 5 pax

Ingredients

- 1/2 teaspoon salt
- 1 (1-inch) piece fresh ginger, cut thin
- 1/4 teaspoon crudely ground black pepper
- 1 teaspoon Chaat Masala
- 1 teaspoon cumin seeds
- 1/2 cup water
- 1 large clove fresh garlic, minced
- 1 large, firm tomato, finely chopped
- 1 tablespoon ground coriander
- 2 tablespoons fresh lemon juice
- 2 cups frozen shelled soybeans, thawed
- 3 cups finely chopped dark green lettuce,
- 4 scallions, minced

Procedure

1. Place the soybeans and water in a microwave-safe dish. Cook in the microwave on high power 5 to 6 minutes, or until the beans are very soft to the touch.
2. Put the lettuce, tomato, and scallion in a big serving container.
3. Heat the oil in a moderate-sized non-stick saucepan using moderate to high heat and put in the ginger and cumin seeds; they should sizzle when they touch the hot oil.
4. Swiftly add first the garlic, coriander, and black pepper, then the soybeans, the rest of the cooking water, and salt.
5. Cover and cook, stirring and swaying the pan, until the soybeans are coated thoroughly, approximately five minutes.
6. Move to the container with the lettuce, tomato and scallion, and put in the lemon juice and chaat masala.
7. Toss and serve warm or at room temperature.

Taro Salad

Serves 5 pax

Ingredients

- 1/2 teaspoon Chaat Masala
- 1/4 teaspoon salt
- 1/2 teaspoon ajwain seeds, crudely ground
- 3 tablespoons finely chopped fresh cilantro
- 8 small taro roots (about 1 pound)
- 1 green chile pepper, minced with seeds
- 1 tablespoon minced fresh mint leaves
- 2 tablespoons fresh lime juice

Procedure

1. In a medium pot, cover the taro root with water, bring to boil, and cook until tender, approximately fifteen minutes.
2. Allow to cool slightly, then peel and cut into 1/2-inch pieces.
3. Put in a serving container and stir in all the rest of the ingredients.
4. Serve warm or at room temperature.

Toasted Orzo Mix

Ingredients

- 1 fennel bulb
- 1/2 cup pitted kalamata olives, chopped
- 3/4 cup dry white wine
- 1 onion, chopped fine
- 1 teaspoon grated orange zest
- 2 cups water
- 3 tablespoons extra-virgin olive oil
- 2 cups orzo
- A pinch of ground nutmeg
- A pinch of red pepper flakes
- 2 ounces Parmesan cheese, grated
- 2 cups chicken or vegetable broth
- 2 garlic cloves, minced
- Salt and pepper

Procedure

1. Heat oil in 12-inch non-stick frying pan on moderate heat until it starts to shimmer. Put in onion and 3/4 teaspoon salt and cook till they become tender and lightly browned, 5 to 7 minutes.
2. Mix in garlic, orange zest, fennel seeds, and pepper flakes and cook until aromatic, approximately half a minute.
1 Put in orzo and cook, stirring often, until orzo is coated with oil and lightly browned, approximately five minutes.
3. Mix in broth, water, and wine and bring to boil. Cook, stirring intermittently, until all liquid has been absorbed and orzo is tender, 10 to fifteen minutes.
4. Mix in olives, Parmesan, and nutmeg and sprinkle with salt and pepper to taste.
5. Serve.

Lemoned Onion Rings

Ingredients

- 1/2 teaspoon hot red pepper flakes
- 6 small red onions, cut into rings
- 1 teaspoon Basic Ginger Paste
- 1/2 cup finely chopped fresh cilantro
- 3 tablespoons fresh lemon juice
- 2 teaspoons salt

Procedure

1. In a non-reactive container, place the onions, put in the salt, and toss well.
2. Cover and let marinate approximately two hours at room temperature.
3. Next, pour into a fine-mesh strainer and drain all the juices and salt (or wash under running water and then drain).
4. Move to a serving container and stir in the cilantro, lemon juice, ginger paste, and red pepper flakes.
5. Cover and place in your fridge for approximately two hours in the fridge to marinate.
6. Serve chilled.

Cabbages and Mung Salad

Serves 5 pax

Ingredients

- 1/2 teaspoon salt
- 1 cup finely chopped onion
- 1 cup thinly shredded green cabbage
- 1 cup thinly shredded red cabbage
- 1/4 cup crudely chopped roasted peanuts
- 2 cups sprouted green mung beans
- 2 tablespoons fresh lime juice
- 3 small tomatoes, each cut into 6 to 8 wedges
- Freshly ground black pepper to taste
- 1/4 cup fresh orange juice
- 1/2 cup finely chopped fresh cilantro
- 1 fresh green chile pepper, minced with seeds
- 1 tablespoon peeled minced fresh ginger

- 1 tablespoon sesame seeds
- 1 teaspoon Chaat Masala
- 2 cups mixed baby greens

Procedure

1. In a container, mix everything except the sesame seeds, baby greens, and peanuts. Cover and marinate at least two hours in a fridge.
2. Mound the mixture over a bed of baby greens, scatter the sesame seeds and peanuts on top before you serve.

Yogurt and Potatoes Salad

Serves 5 pax

Ingredients

- 1/2 teaspoon salt
- 1 cup yogurt, whisked
- 1 tablespoon peeled minced fresh ginger
- 1/4 cup finely chopped fresh cilantro
- 2 tablespoons peanut oil
- 8 scallions, white parts only, finely chopped
- 1/4 teaspoon freshly ground black pepper
- 1/4 teaspoon salt
- 2 green chile peppers, minced with seeds
- 2 pounds russet potatoes, peeled or unpeeled
- 2 teaspoons cumin seeds

Procedure

1. In a medium pan, cover the potatoes with water, bring to a boil, and cook until tender, approximately fifteen minutes.
2. Drain, allow to cool, then cut into 3/4-inch pieces.
3. In a moderate-sized container, combine the yogurt, salt, black pepper, and scallions.
4. Heat the oil in a big skillet using moderate to high heat and lightly cook the potatoes, stirring, approximately three minutes.
5. Put in the ginger, green chile peppers, cilantro, and salt, and cook, turning as required, until the potatoes are golden on all sides, approximately five minutes.
6. Move to a serving dish and drizzle the yogurt sauce and half the roasted cumin over the potatoes. Mix lightly.
7. Garnish with the rest of the cumin and serve.

2 Potatoes and Peas Salad

Serves 5 pax

Ingredients

- 1/2 pound small, pale-fleshed sweet potatoes
- 1/2 teaspoon cayenne pepper
- 1/2 teaspoon salt
- 1 pound small white potatoes
- 3 tablespoons peanut oil
- 4 tablespoons Tamarind Paste
- 1/2 cup finely chopped fresh cilantro
- 1/2 cup finely chopped sweet onion
- 1/2 to 1 teaspoon Chaat Masala
- 1 cup peas, thawed

Procedure

1. In separate pots, cover the white potatoes and sweet potatoes in lightly salted water, bring to a boil, and cook until tender, approximately fifteen minutes for the potatoes and fifteen to twenty minutes for the sweet potatoes (depending on their thickness).

2. Drain and allow to cool down, then peel all the potatoes. Cut each white potato in half lengthwise and cut the sweet potatoes into thick rounds.

3. In a large cast-iron or non-stick skillet, heat the oil using moderate to high heat and cook the white potatoes and sweet potatoes until a golden color is achieved brown on both sides, approximately seven minutes, turning as required.

4. As you cook them, press each piece with the back of the spatula to flatten it as much as possible.

6. Move to a plate, and when they are cool sufficient to handle, use clean fingers to crudely break each piece into 2 or 3 smaller pieces.
7. Put in the peas to the same skillet and cook using moderate to high heat, stirring, until barely golden, approximately four minutes. Mix the potatoes and sweet potatoes into the peas.
8. Next, put in the tamarind paste, salt, cayenne pepper, chaat masala, and cilantro and cook, turning a few times as required, approximately two minutes.
9. Adjust seasonings, adding more salt, chaat masala, or tamarind, if required.
10. Move to a serving platter, top with the chopped onions before you serve.

Potatoes Masala Salad

Serves 5 pax

Ingredients

- 1 green chile pepper, minced with seeds
- 1 tablespoon minced fresh mint leaves
- 1/2 cup finely chopped fresh cilantro
- 2 teaspoons Chaat Masala
- 2 tablespoons olive oil
- 3 tablespoons fresh lemon juice
- 1/2 teaspoon salt
- 1 teaspoon cumin seeds
- 2 pounds small red potatoes, unpeeled
- 2 teaspoons grated lemon peel (zest)

Procedure

1. In a medium pot, cover the potatoes with water, bring to a boil, and cook until tender, approximately fifteen minutes. Drain, allow to cool down, then cut into 1/2-inch pieces. (Do not remove the skin.)

2. In a large skillet, heat the oil using moderate to high heat and add first the cumin seeds, then the lemon peel, mint, and green chile pepper. Cook, shaking the skillet, approximately half a minute.

3. Put in the potatoes and salt and cook, flipping the potatoes as required, until a golden color is achieved on all sides, approximately seven minutes. Decrease the heat if they begin to brown too swiftly.

4. Put in the cilantro and lemon juice, cook another minute, then stir in half the chaat masala. Move to a serving dish.

5. Sprinkle with the rest of the chaat masala and serve warm or at room temperature.

Sweet Potatoes Salad

Serves 5 pax

Ingredients

- 1 green chile pepper, minced with seeds
- 1/4 cup finely chopped fresh cilantro
- 1/2 teaspoon salt
- 2 tablespoons Tamarind Paste
- 1 sweet potatoes (about 1 pound)
- 1 tablespoon brown sugar
- 1 tablespoon peeled minced fresh ginger
- 1 teaspoon cumin seeds

Procedure

1. In a large pot, cover the sweet potatoes with water, bring to a boil, and cook until tender, approximately fifteen minutes.
2. Allow to cool, then peel and cut into 3/4-inch pieces.
3. Put in a serving container and stir in all the rest of the ingredients.
4. Cover and refrigerate approximately one hour to serve chilled.

Gingered Shrimps Salad

Serves 5 pax

Ingredients

- 1 (1-inch) piece fresh ginger, peeled and cut
- 1 each of red and yellow bell peppers, cut
- 1/2 teaspoon salt
- 1 large clove fresh garlic, minced
- 2 cups mixed baby greens
- 3 tablespoons fresh lemon juice
- 2 tablespoons minced fresh mint leaves
- 2 tablespoons vegetable oil
- 4 scallions, white parts only, thinly chopped
- 1 pound shrimp (about 20), shelled and deveined
- 1 small seedless cucumber cut into thin 11/2-inches
- 1 teaspoon crudely ground ajwain seeds
- 1 teaspoon Chaat Masala

Procedure

1. Put the shrimp in a big non-reactive container. Put in the ginger, garlic, lime juice, ajwain seeds, salt and mix thoroughly, ensuring all the shrimp are coated thoroughly with the marinade.
2. Refrigerate approximately two hours.
3. Heat the oil in a big non-stick wok or saucepan using moderate to high heat and cook the mint leaves, stirring, approximately half a minute.
4. Put in the shrimp and the marinade and cook until the shrimp are pink, approximately three minutes.
5. In a large container, combine the greens, bell peppers, and cucumber, and toss with the chaat masala. Move to a serving platter.
6. Scatter the cooked shrimp over the greens, top with the scallions before you serve.

Chicken and Lentils Salad

Serves 5 pax

Ingredients

- 1 fresh green chile pepper, minced with seeds
- 1 large onion, finely chopped
- 1/2 cup yogurt, whisked
- 1 large russet potato, unpeeled
- 1 pound boneless, skinless chicken breasts, minced
- 1 red bell pepper, finely chopped
- 1 tablespoon peeled minced fresh ginger
- 2 tablespoons fresh lime juice
- 2 tablespoons vegetable oil
- 6 Spicy Lentil Wafers
- 1 teaspoon dried fenugreek leaves
- 1 teaspoon garam masala
- 1 teaspoon salt

Procedure

1. In a small pan, cover the potato with water, bring to a boil, and cook until tender, approximately ten minutes. Allow to cool, then peel, finely chop, and save for later.

2. In a non-stick saucepan, heat the oil using moderate to high heat and cook the chicken, onion, ginger, green chile pepper, garam masala, fenugreek leaves, and salt, stirring to break most of the lumps, until the chicken is golden, approximately five minutes.

3. Add all the yogurt at once and cook until most of the liquid has evaporated and the yogurt is absorbed, approximately five minutes.

4. Stir in the lime juice, red bell pepper, potato and cook another 3 minutes. Allow to cool.

5. In the meantime, ready the paapads.

6. Move the chicken and vegetables to a serving platter. Break the paapads into small pieces and place them around the chicken.

7. Serve.

Spinaches Salad

Serves 5 pax

Ingredients

- 1 tablespoon melted honey
- 1/2 teaspoon salt
- 1 cup yogurt, whisked
- 1 teaspoon peanut oil
- 2 teaspoons cumin seeds
- 2 cups firmly packed baby spinach leaves, trimmed, washed well and spin-dried
- Freshly ground black pepper to taste
- 1/2 teaspoon ground ginger
- 1 tablespoon fresh lemon juice

Procedure

1. Place the spinach leaves in a salad container.
2. Heat the oil in a small saucepan and add first the ginger, then the lemon juice and honey, and stir to mix.
3. Turn off the heat and allow to cool down. Stir in the yogurt, 1 teaspoon cumin seeds, salt, and black pepper.
4. Put into the spinach and toss lightly to mix.
5. Sprinkle the rest of the cumin seeds on top and serve.

Tandoori Chicken Salad

Serves 5 pax

Ingredients

- 1 (2- to 21/2-pound) Grilled Tandoori Chicken
- 1 large tomato, cut into 1/2-inch pieces
- 1 teaspoon Chaat Masala
- 1/4 cup finely chopped fresh cilantro
- 1 (1-inch) piece peeled fresh ginger, cut into thin
- 1 teaspoon cumin seeds
- 3 small seedless cucumbers, cut into 1/2-inch pieces
- 3 tablespoons fresh lemon or lime juice
- 8 scallions, white parts only, thinly chopped
- 2 green chile peppers, minced with seeds
- 2 tablespoons vegetable oil
- 2 tablespoons minced fresh mint leaves

Procedure

1. Ready the tandoori chicken, then pull the meat off the bone and shred it. Ready the cumin seeds and the chaat masala.
2. In a serving container, combine the shredded chicken, tomato, cucumbers, scallions, and cilantro.
3. Heat the oil in a small-sized non-stick saucepan using moderate to high heat and cook the ginger, stirring, until a golden color is achieved, approximately three minutes.
4. Stir in the green chile peppers and mint and stir approximately one minute.
5. Put in the lemon juice and chaat masala and stir a few seconds. Put into the chicken and mix thoroughly. Taste and adjust the seasonings.
6. Sprinkle with the roasted cumin and serve.

Thanks

To all of you who arrived until here.

I am glad you accepted my teachings.
These have been my personal meals in the past years, so I wished to share them with you.

Now you had come to know about Mediterranean and Indian Salads, let me give you one more tip.
This manual takes part of an unmissable cookbooks collection.
These salad-based recipes, mixed to all the tastes I met in my worldwide journeys, will give you a complete idea of the possibilities this world offers to us.
You have now the opportunity to add hundreds new elements to your cooking skills knowledge.
Check out the other books!

CPSIA information can be obtained
at www.ICGtesting.com
Printed in the USA
BVHW041101130521
607269BV00012B/2511